THE WEALTH PRINCIPLES

Unveiling The Principles of Financial Success

Elon Philips

Copyright © 2023 Elon Philips

Contents

INTRODUCTION

Chapter 1
Setting the Stage for Financial prosperity

Chapter 2
Understanding the Fundamentals of Business Investing

Chapter 3
Building a Strong Financial **Portfolio**

Chapter 4

Creating a Money Generating Plan

Chapter 5

Improving Your Earnings Capacity

Chapter 6
Reducing Your Tax Liability

Chapter 7
Proper Risk Control

Chapter 8

Investment Diversification

Chapter 9
Ideas For Wealth Preservation

Chapter 10
Retirement Plans

Chapter 11
Family Financial Plan

Chapter 12
Legacy Planning and Generational Wealth

Chapter 13

Strategic Business Management

INTRODUCTION

Unlocking the Secrets of Financial Success" is a comprehensive guide to achieving financial freedom. Written by a team of experienced financial experts, this book will teach you the secrets of building wealth and achieving your financial goals. Whether you're a beginner or an experienced investor, this book will provide you with the tools and strategies you need to succeed. From understanding the basics of investing to advanced wealth-building techniques, "The Wealth Code" is your ultimate guide to financial success. With clear, concise, and actionable advice, this book will show you how to take control of your finances and create the life you've always wanted. So, if you're ready to take the first step towards financial freedom, open the book and let's begin the journey together.

Chapter 1

Setting the Stage for Financial prosperity

Welcome to "The Wealth Code: Unlocking the Secrets of Financial Success." This book is designed to provide you with the knowledge and tools you need to achieve financial freedom and build long-term wealth. In this chapter, we will set the stage for your financial journey by discussing the importance of financial literacy and the key principles of wealth building.

The first step towards achieving financial success is understanding the importance of financial literacy. Financial literacy is the ability to understand and manage one's finances effectively. It includes knowledge of basic financial concepts, such as budgeting, saving, investing, and managing debt. Without financial literacy, it is difficult to make informed decisions about your money and achieve your financial goals.

In addition to financial literacy, the key principles of wealth building are discipline, patience, and consistency. Building wealth takes time and effort, and it requires a long-term perspective. It is important to have a clear plan in place and to stick to it, even when faced with setbacks or challenges. The discipline to save and invest regularly, the patience to wait for your investments to grow, and the consistency to stick to your plan are all essential for building wealth.

Furthermore, it is important to understand that financial freedom is not just about having a lot of money. It is about having the ability to live the life you want without worrying about money. It's about being able to make choices and pursue your passions without financial constraints.

In this book, we will explore various strategies for building wealth and achieving financial freedom. We will discuss everything from the basics of investing to advanced wealth-building techniques. We will also delve into the psychology of wealth and explore the mindset and habits that are essential for financial success.

In summary, financial literacy, discipline, patience, consistency and understanding the concept of financial freedom are the key ingredients for setting the stage for financial success. This chapter serves as a foundation for the rest of the book and will provide you with the knowledge and mindset you need to start your journey towards financial freedom.

Chapter 2

Understanding the Fundamentals of Business Investing

In this chapter, we will discuss the basics of investing, including the different types of investments, the importance of diversification, and the role of risk in investing. Understanding these concepts is essential for building a strong investment portfolio and achieving your financial goals.

The first step in understanding investing is to understand the different types of investments. Some common types of investments include stocks, bonds, mutual funds, real estate, and precious metals. Each type of investment has its own unique characteristics and risks, and it's important to understand the differences in order to make informed investment decisions.

Stocks, for example, are a type of equity investment that represents ownership in a company. When you buy a stock, you are essentially buying a small piece of the company. The value of your investment will fluctuate based on the performance of the company. Stocks have the potential for high returns, but they also come with a higher level of risk.

Bonds, on the other hand, are a type of debt investment. When you buy a bond, you are essentially lending money to the issuer of the bond, such as a government or corporation. The issuer agrees to pay you back the principal plus interest over a set period of time. Bonds tend to be less risky than stocks, but they also have lower returns.

Another important concept in investing is diversification. Diversification refers to spreading your money across different types of investments in order to reduce risk. By diversifying your portfolio, you can reduce the impact of any one investment performing poorly. For example, if your entire portfolio is invested in one company, and that company's stock drops, your entire portfolio will be affected. However, if your portfolio is diversified across different companies, sectors, and assets classes, the impact of one company's stock dropping will be less severe.

Another important aspect of investing is understanding and managing risk. Investing always involves some level of risk, and it's important to understand how much risk you're comfortable taking on. Some investments, such as stocks, tend to be riskier than others, such as bonds. It's important to understand the risk profile of each investment and to diversify your portfolio in order to manage risk.

In summary, understanding the basics of investing is essential for building a strong investment portfolio and achieving your financial goals. By understanding the different types of investments, the importance of diversification, and the role of risk in investing, you can make informed decisions and create a portfolio that aligns with your risk tolerance and financial goals.

Chapter 3

Building a Strong Financial Portfolio

In this chapter, we will discuss the importance of building a strong financial foundation and the key elements that are required to achieve this. A strong financial foundation is the foundation on which you can build long-term wealth and achieve financial freedom.

The first element of a strong financial foundation is having a budget. A budget is a plan for how you will spend your money. It helps you to understand your income and expenses, and to make sure that you are saving enough to reach your financial goals. Without a budget, it is easy to overspend and fall into debt.

The second element of a strong financial foundation is having an emergency fund. An emergency fund is a savings account that is set aside for unexpected expenses, such as a job loss or medical emergency. Having an emergency fund can help to provide peace of mind, knowing that you have a safety net in place in case of unexpected events.

The third element of a strong financial foundation is paying off high-interest debt. High-interest debt, such as credit card debt, can be a major obstacle to achieving financial freedom. The interest on this type of debt can add up quickly, making it difficult to get ahead. Paying off high-interest debt is an important step in building a strong financial foundation.

The fourth element of a strong financial foundation is having a savings plan. A savings plan is a plan for how you will save money, and it should include a specific savings goal. This could be for retirement, a down payment on a house, or a child's education. Having a savings plan helps to ensure that you are saving enough to reach your goals.

Finally, having a good credit score is the fifth key element of a strong financial foundation. A good credit score is essential for getting approved for loans and credit, and it can also affect the interest rate you are offered. A good credit score is a reflection of your financial responsibility and it can save you money in the long run.

In summary, building a strong financial foundation is essential for achieving long-term wealth and financial freedom. A budget, emergency fund, paying off high-interest debt, having a savings plan and having a good credit score are the key elements of a strong financial foundation. By focusing on these elements, you can create a solid foundation for your financial future.

Chapter 4
Creating a Money Generating Plan

In this chapter, we will discuss the importance of having a wealth-building plan and the key elements of such a plan. A wealth-building plan is a comprehensive strategy for achieving financial freedom and building long-term wealth.

The first element of a wealth-building plan is setting clear and specific financial goals. These goals should be specific, measurable, achievable, relevant, and time-bound (SMART). Setting clear and specific financial goals will help to keep you motivated and focused on what you want to achieve.

The second element of a wealth-building plan is to identify your risk tolerance. Risk tolerance is the level of risk you are willing to take on when it comes to investments. Understanding your risk tolerance will help you to make informed investment decisions and to create a diversified portfolio that aligns with your risk tolerance.

The third element of a wealth-building plan is to develop a savings and investment strategy. This strategy should include both short-term and long-term goals, such as saving for a down payment on a house, retirement, or a child's education. It should also include a plan for how you will invest your money, including a mix of different types of investments to diversify your portfolio.

The fourth element of a wealth-building plan is to create a plan for managing debt. This includes paying off high-interest debt, such as credit card debt, and developing a plan for managing other types of debt, such as student loans or a mortgage.

The fifth element of a wealth-building plan is to periodically review and adjust your plan. As your life and financial situation change, your wealth-building plan should be reviewed and adjusted accordingly. This will help you to stay on track and make sure that your plan is aligned with your current financial goals and situation.

In summary, having a wealth-building plan is essential for achieving financial freedom and building long-term wealth. A wealth-building plan should include clear and specific financial goals, identification of your risk tolerance, a savings and investment strategy, a plan for managing debt, and regular review and adjustments. By focusing on these elements, you can create a comprehensive strategy for achieving your financial goals.

Chapter 5

Improving Your Earnings Capacity

In this chapter, we will discuss the importance of maximizing your earning potential and the various strategies for doing so. Maximizing your earning potential is an essential part of building long-term wealth and achieving financial freedom.

The first strategy for maximizing your earning potential is to continuously invest in your education and skills. The more knowledge and skills you have, the more valuable you will be in the workforce and the more earning potential you will have. This can include traditional education such as college or vocational school, or self-education through online resources and workshops.

Another strategy for maximizing your earning potential is to seek out new and higher paying job opportunities. This can include looking for promotions within your current company or seeking out new job opportunities with better pay and benefits. Networking and building professional relationships can also be a great way to learn about new job opportunities.

Entrepreneurship is another way to maximize your earning potential. Starting your own business can be a great way to increase your income and gain financial freedom. This can include starting a small business, investing in a franchise, or becoming a freelancer or consultant.

Investing in assets that generate passive income can also be a great way to maximize your earning potential. This can include investments such as rental properties, dividend-paying stocks, or peer-to-peer lending. Passive income streams can provide a regular source of income without the need for active involvement.

Finally, negotiation is an important skill to have when it

comes to maximizing your earning potential. Whether it's negotiating a higher salary, better benefits, or more flexible working conditions, being able to negotiate effectively can help you to increase your income.

In summary, maximizing your earning potential is an essential part of building long-term wealth and achieving financial freedom. Investing in your education and skills, seeking out new and higher-paying job opportunities, entrepreneurship, investing in assets that generate passive income, and negotiation are all effective strategies for maximizing your earning potential. By focusing on these strategies, you can increase your income and achieve your financial goals.

Chapter 6

Reducing Your Tax Liability

In this chapter, we will discuss the importance of minimizing your tax liability and the various strategies for doing so. Minimizing your tax liability is an essential part of achieving financial freedom and building long-term wealth.

The first strategy for minimizing your tax liability is to stay informed about the tax laws and regulations that apply to you. By staying up-to-date with the latest tax laws and regulations, you can take advantage of deductions, credits, and other tax-saving strategies that can help to lower your tax bill.

Another strategy for minimizing your tax liability is to take advantage of deductions and credits. Deductions and credits can help to lower your taxable income, and thereby reduce your tax liability. Some common deductions include mortgage interest, state and local taxes, and charitable donations. Some common credits include the Child Tax Credit, the Earned Income Tax Credit, and the American Opportunity Tax Credit.

Investing in tax-advantaged accounts, such as 401(k)s,

IRAs, and HSAs, can also help to minimize your tax liability. These types of accounts allow you to save and invest for retirement or healthcare expenses while also receiving tax benefits.

Maximizing your deductions and credits through proper tax planning and itemizing your deductions can also help to minimize your tax liability. This can include taking advantage of deductions for business expenses, medical expenses, and education expenses.

Finally, hiring a tax professional can be a great way to minimize your tax liability. A tax professional can help you to take advantage of all the deductions and credits that apply to you and can ensure that your tax return is filed correctly and on time.

In summary, minimizing your tax liability is an essential

part of achieving financial freedom and building long-term wealth. Staying informed about tax laws and regulations, taking advantage of deductions and credits, investing in tax-advantaged accounts, maximizing deductions and credits through proper tax planning, and hiring a tax professional are all effective strategies for minimizing your tax liability. By focusing on these strategies, you can lower your tax bill and keep more of your money to invest and save for your future.

Chapter 7

Proper Risk Control

In this chapter, we will discuss the importance of understanding and managing risk in the context of investing and building wealth. Understanding and managing risk is essential for achieving financial freedom and building long-term wealth.

The first step in understanding and managing risk is to understand the different types of risk that are associated with investing. These include market risk, credit risk, liquidity risk, and inflation risk. Market risk, for example, is the risk that the value of an investment will decrease due to changes in the market. Credit risk, on the other hand, is the risk that a borrower will default on a loan. Understanding the different types of risk can help you to make informed investment decisions.

The second step in understanding and managing risk is to understand your own risk tolerance. Risk tolerance is the level of risk that you are comfortable taking on when it comes to investments. Everyone's risk tolerance is different, and it's important to understand your own risk tolerance in order to make informed investment decisions.

The third step in understanding and managing risk is to create a diversified portfolio. Diversification is a risk management strategy that involves spreading your investments across different types of investments, such as stocks, bonds, and real estate. By diversifying your portfolio, you can reduce the impact of any one investment performing poorly.

Another strategy for managing risk is to have a long-term investment horizon. Long-term investing allows you to ride out short-term market fluctuations and can help to reduce the risk of your investments. It also allows your investments to grow over time.

Finally, it's important to have a plan in place to manage risk. This can include setting stop-losses, re-balancing your portfolio periodically and reviewing your investment strategy regularly.

In summary, understanding and managing risk is essential for achieving financial freedom and building long-term wealth. By understanding the different types of risk, understanding your own risk tolerance, creating a diversified portfolio, having a long-term investment horizon, and having a plan in place to manage risk, you can make informed investment decisions and protect your wealth.

Chapter 8

Investment Diversification

In this chapter, we will discuss the importance of building a diversified investment portfolio and the various strategies for doing so. A diversified investment portfolio is a portfolio that includes a mix of different types of investments, such as stocks, bonds, real estate, and precious metals. Building a diversified portfolio is essential for achieving financial freedom and building long-term wealth.

The first step in building a diversified portfolio is to understand the different types of investments and their characteristics. This includes understanding the risk, return, and volatility of different types of investments, as well as their potential for growth. By understanding the different types of investments, you can make informed decisions about which investments to include in your portfolio.

The second step in building a diversified portfolio is to create a mix of different types of investments. This includes a mix of stocks, bonds, and cash, as well as alternative investments such as real estate, precious metals, and private equity. By diversifying your portfolio across different types of investments, you can reduce the impact of any one investment performing poorly.

Another strategy for building a diversified portfolio is to diversify within each asset class. This can include diversifying across different sectors, such as technology, healthcare, and energy, as well as diversifying across different geographic regions, such as the US, Europe, and Asia.

Rebalancing your portfolio periodically is also an important aspect of building a diversified portfolio. This means adjusting the mix of investments in your portfolio to ensure that it aligns with your financial goals and risk tolerance.

Finally, it's important to review your portfolio regularly and make adjustments as necessary. This can include monitoring the performance of your investments, making changes to the mix of investments in your portfolio, and ensuring that your portfolio is aligned with your financial goals and risk tolerance.

In summary, building a diversified investment portfolio is essential for achieving financial freedom and building long-term wealth. By understanding the different types of investments and their characteristics, creating a mix of different types of investments, diversifying within each asset class, rebalancing your portfolio periodically, and reviewing your portfolio regularly, you can create a diversified portfolio that aligns with your financial goals and risk tolerance. By diversifying your portfolio, you can reduce the impact of any one investment performing poorly and achieve a balance between risk and return.

Chapter 9

Ideas For Wealth Preservation

In this chapter, we will discuss the various strategies for building and preserving wealth. Building and preserving wealth is essential for achieving financial freedom and creating a secure financial future.

The first strategy for building and preserving wealth is to live below your means. This means spending less than you earn and saving and investing the difference. Living below your means is the foundation upon which wealth can be built.

The second strategy for building and preserving wealth is to invest in assets that appreciate in value. This includes investments such as stocks, real estate, and businesses. These types of investments have the potential to grow in value over time, which can help to build and preserve wealth.

Another strategy for building and preserving wealth is to minimize taxes. Minimizing taxes can help to keep more of your money to invest and save for the future. This can include taking advantage of deductions and credits, investing in tax-advantaged accounts, and seeking out professional tax advice.

Having a long-term investment horizon is also an important aspect of building and preserving wealth. This means investing for the long term, rather than trying to time the market or make quick profits. Long-term investing allows you to ride out short-term market fluctuations and can help to build and preserve wealth over time.

Finally, it's important to have a plan in place to manage risk. This can include setting stop-losses, diversifying your portfolio, and reviewing your investment strategy regularly.

In summary, building and preserving wealth is essential for achieving financial freedom and creating a secure financial future. By living below your means, investing in assets that appreciate in value, minimizing taxes, having a long-term investment horizon, and managing risk, you can build and preserve wealth over time. By focusing on these strategies, you can create a solid foundation for your financial future and achieve your financial goals.

Chapter 10

Retirement Plans

In this chapter, we will discuss the importance of planning for retirement and the various strategies for doing so. Planning for retirement is an essential part of achieving financial freedom and building long-term wealth.

The first step in planning for retirement is to understand the different types of retirement accounts and the benefits they offer. These include 401(k)s, IRAs, and Roth IRAs. Understanding the different types of accounts and the benefits they offer can help you to make informed decisions about how to save for retirement.

The second step in planning for retirement is to start saving early and consistently. The earlier you start saving for retirement, the more time your money has to grow and compound. Consistently saving a portion of your income can also help to ensure that you have enough saved for retirement.

Another strategy for planning for retirement is to invest in a diversified portfolio. This includes a mix of stocks, bonds, and cash, as well as alternative investments such as real estate, precious metals, and private equity. A diversified portfolio can help to reduce the impact of any one investment performing poorly, and can help to maximize returns over time.

Creating a retirement budget and planning for retirement expenses is also an important aspect of planning for retirement. This means estimating how much you'll need to live on in retirement and planning for expenses such as healthcare and travel.

Finally, it's important to review and adjust your retirement plan regularly as your life and financial situation change. This can include adjusting your savings goals and investment strategy, as well as re-evaluating your retirement budget and expenses.

In summary, planning for retirement is an essential part of achieving financial freedom and building long-term wealth. By understanding the different types of retirement accounts, starting to save early and consistently, investing in a diversified portfolio, creating a retirement budget, and regularly reviewing and adjusting your plan, you can create a comprehensive strategy for achieving your retirement goals. By focusing on these strategies, you can ensure that you have enough saved for a comfortable retirement and enjoy your golden years with peace of mind.

Chapter 11

Family Financial Plan

In this chapter, we will discuss the importance of financial planning for families and the various strategies for doing so. Financial planning for families is essential for achieving financial freedom and building long-term wealth.

The first step in financial planning for families is to set clear and specific financial goals. These goals should be specific, measurable, achievable, relevant, and time-bound (SMART) and should be tailored to the unique needs of your family. Setting clear and specific financial goals will help to keep your family focused on what they want to achieve.

The second step in financial planning for families is to

create a budget. This means understanding your income and expenses and creating a plan for managing your money. A budget can help you to prioritize your spending and ensure that you have enough money to meet your financial goals.

Another strategy for financial planning for families is to invest in a diversified portfolio. This includes a mix of stocks, bonds, and cash, as well as alternative investments such as real estate, precious metals, and private equity. A diversified portfolio can help to reduce the impact of any one investment performing poorly and can help to maximize returns over time.

Providing financial education for your children is also an important aspect of financial planning for families. This means teaching your children about money, budgeting, saving, investing, and other important financial concepts.

Finally, it's important to review and adjust your financial plan regularly as your family's life and financial situation change. This can include adjusting your savings goals and investment strategy, as well as re-evaluating your budget and expenses.

In summary, financial planning for families is

essential for achieving financial freedom and building long-term wealth. By setting clear and specific financial goals, creating a budget, investing in a diversified portfolio, providing financial education for your children, and regularly reviewing and adjusting your plan, you can create a comprehensive strategy for achieving your family's financial goals. By focusing on these strategies, you can ensure that your family has the financial resources they need to thrive and enjoy a secure financial future.

Chapter 12

Legacy Planning and Generational Wealth

In this chapter, we will discuss the importance of legacy planning and estate planning and the various strategies for doing so. Legacy planning and estate planning are essential for ensuring that your assets and wealth are passed on to your loved ones in the way you intend, and for minimizing taxes and legal issues.

The first step in legacy planning and estate planning is to create a will. A will is a legal document that outlines how your assets will be distributed after your death. It can also include instructions for the care of any minor children or dependents.

The second step in legacy planning and estate planning is to set up a trust. A trust is a legal entity that can hold assets on behalf of beneficiaries. Trusts can be used for a variety of purposes, such as minimizing taxes, protecting assets from creditors, and providing for the care of dependents.

Another strategy for legacy planning and estate planning is to create a power of attorney. A power of attorney is a legal document that allows you to appoint someone to make financial and legal decisions on your behalf in case you become incapacitated.

Designating beneficiaries on your accounts and insurance policies is also an important aspect of legacy planning and estate planning. This means ensuring that the beneficiaries on your accounts and insurance policies align with your will and trust.

Finally, it's important to review and update your legacy planning and estate planning documents regularly. This can include updating your will and trust, changing beneficiaries on accounts and insurance policies, and ensuring that your power of attorney is up-to-date.

In summary, legacy planning and estate planning are essential for ensuring that your assets and wealth are passed on to your loved ones in the way you intend, and for minimizing taxes and legal issues. By creating a will, setting up a trust, creating a power of attorney, designating beneficiaries, and regularly reviewing and updating your documents, you can create a comprehensive strategy for passing on your legacy and protecting your assets for future generations. By focusing on these strategies, you can ensure that your loved ones are taken care of and that your legacy lives on.

Chapter 13

Strategic Business Management

In this chapter, we will discuss the importance of building and managing a business and the various strategies for doing so. Building and managing a business can be a powerful way to achieve financial freedom and build long-term wealth.

The first step in building and managing a business is to identify a profitable business idea. This means researching the market and identifying a need that your business can meet. It also means assessing your own skills and interests to determine if you are a good fit for the business you are considering.

The second step in building and managing a business is to create a business plan. A business plan is a document that outlines your business idea, target market, financial projections, and strategy for achieving your goals. A solid business plan can help you to secure funding and attract investors.

Another strategy for building and managing a business is to build a strong team. This means hiring the right people to help you run your business and build a team that is skilled, dedicated, and committed to your success.

Marketing and promoting your business is also an important aspect of building and managing a business. This means developing a marketing strategy that will help you to reach your target market and attract customers.

Finally, it's important to regularly review and adjust your business plan. This can include analyzing your financial performance, assessing the effectiveness of your marketing strategy, and making changes to your operations as needed.

In summary, building and managing a business can be a powerful way to achieve financial freedom and build long-term wealth. By identifying a profitable business idea, creating a business plan, building a strong team, marketing and promoting your business, and regularly reviewing and adjusting your plan, you can create a comprehensive strategy for building and managing a successful business. By focusing on these strategies, you can turn your business idea into a thriving enterprise and achieve your financial goals.

www.ingramcontent.com/pod-product-compliance
Lightning Source LLC
Chambersburg PA
CBHW050331220526
45465CB00018B/1520